ABOUT THE AUTHOR

Catherine Balaq is a writer and body psychotherapist. She is co-editor of Black Cat Press. Her debut collection *animaginary* was published in 2023. *Deathless* is her second collection. Catherine also writes novels and is represented by Donald Winchester at Watson Little.

ABOUT *Deathless*

'Catherine Balaq channels the daemon onto the page summoning colour from darkness.' **Paul Lynch**

'Intimate, open-hearted and blazingly honest, the poems in *Deathless* establish Balacq as a distinctive and engaging voice. Memory and survival; wit and invention; duty and wild abandon. It captures the beautiful and terrifying simultaneity of life: all of this is happening at once, is behind us, is coming our way.' **Luke Kennard**

'*Deathless* tracks the nuances of female desire, its ambivalences and contradictions, celebrating its incendiary agency with precision and control.' **Meryl Pugh**

'Balaq's words leaves you breathless, burning through the page, reaching into the depths of you and making no apology for it. In *Deathless* we are confronted with the complex, beautiful and exhilarating nature of being alive.' **Ophira Adar**

Death*less*
Catherine Balaq

VERVE
POETRY PRESS
BIRMINGHAM

PUBLISHED BY VERVE POETRY PRESS
https://vervepoetrypress.com
mail@vervepoetrypress.com

FIRST PUBLISHED OCT 2024

Printed and bound in the UK
by ImprintDigital, Exeter

ISBN: 978-1-913917-58-6

Death cannot harm me
more than you have harmed me,
my beloved life.

Louise Glück, Averno

CONTENTS

PART II

Death*less*

Part I

Deprived of death and bereft of life.

-Canto XXXIV, Dante's *Inferno*

.

The Death of Want

so I pull the hood back—pull—drag my skin until I taste death's
teeth—he's looking at me—I want to bite death back

to feel death's breath on the curve of my neck—I want death
to want me—watch me walking through the woods—pull my hair

tight—legs long and booted—I am taller than death—I am more
than his little grief—give myself back to me—more

than this little grief—give yourself back to you—more
tight legs—long and booted—you are taller than death—you are more

to want—watch you walking through the woods—pull your hair
to feel death's breath on the curve of your neck—you want death's

teeth—he's looking at you—you want to bite death back
so you pull the hood back—pull—drag your skin until you taste death

Venus

after Botticelli

She drifts, pearl bone
blessed. In pink lipped
shell, nipple perched
on small peached
breast, gold-haired,
blue eyed. Evoking
spring. Before they hold
her down. She has got it,
yeah baby she's got it—
Kate Bush in toed gold
catsuit, bungling sexy
on piano, concealed
in snake-like skin, a child
in her eyes. Little girls
should be seen and not
heard. This dirty bird
is bad, is rot and slut,
remove her mouth
to shut her up, cut
her clit like fletch
to bone your clout.
Calm down dear. Truth
comes. Cock sick.
Spits flat breast milk,
sapped. Each wound
greater than the last,
forced open, strung out.
Years of cowing,

with stakes and arcs.
Danced on rope.
Left marks. Ducked
in water. Knees worn
stark from bows. Made
from his *bones*? Know
these very ribs already
died. In the garden,
she's a whore to culture:
Adders root, Lords
and Lady leaves.
The tucks and folds
of her flower now
cover scrub hedge,
newsprint flashed on
every raw height:
Page three devils
and *Victoria's Secret* angels.
Time gapes in flesh.
Hips curve, tears splash
down thick thighs.

Wake

after Tamar Yoseloff

To mark the pain you have been searching for gravity
in old photos. Truth? You were born, plucking

black secrets from men as tall as the walls. As in nowhere
else to go. As if you were still there, looking.

What really happened? Remember, it marked
you red (the candle captures your face);

opening. The wound gapes. You squint, through
the mirror you see eyes.

The day is dead. Sleep. Now you light
a memory on the opposite shore.

Look again. Memory
squints through lights. Lies,

see a face marked in pain.
The secret gaping, (as if you were still

captured). What you remember happened.
A room as tall as truth. Searching for walls to mark

the birth, the day, the fact of what is
really dying. Today

the mirror is the near shore. Taking
a photo. Plucking eyes, in silence, like gravity.

Night Car Narcissa

I

Drive your car back along the road.
Emptied lanes in slowed November.
Veins diverting, quivers in your gaunt
metal body from years ago.
Passing into the slick oil of days
without past, flaring hard. A hand encloses
a gasket inside you, always decreasing,
squeezes arteries under pistons
and the crankshaft pushes a spark plug
through the oval opening of the eyes.
You want to drive without passengers,
a rosary swinging from the rear view,
no sign of an oath.

II

Pull over and park. It is getting colder.
Vans with their back doors open.
Behind the scrubby breastbone,
a broken-down caravan on blocks
and someone asks *who lives here?*
Turn off the interior light. Place your hands
across your ribs. You don't want to see
the shadows, but look anyway. The mirror tilted.
You see yourself reflected back infinitum,
filtered face over and over. Hours lurch
forwards with the timing belt. The hands
of the dash clock bind their way around the future.
The air in your lungs, exhausted. *Breathe out.*

III

Undo your seatbelt. Don't fumble. There beneath
knitted nylon it is six o'clock. Darkness has fallen
under belly button and bonnet and the sweated skin
below breasts. In these spaces it is always dark.
Past the headlamps of the bosoms, treadless tyres
of the midriff, marginal knee hubs blossoming silver,
legs fallen wide as a drawn wiper. Open the mound
of Venus, leather ripped taut over foam. The starving
pedals of the labia, limping between the broken axels
of the hips. It's all the grease you ever felt
but are no longer able to give. Unspent it gathers,
caught in the throat. Still your fingers over
the rested key, the centre of you rusting.

Metamorphosis

He sheds bones, breathes through her ribs, lips rattling, clutches her throat. Groans—*it's been on the edge of me all week, it's been a blue moon of not feasting.* Her thighs wrap round a trunk, slough bark with rubbing, smooth as the snake circling, first stirring the garden, *that's it—raise me here, that's it—help me loosen.* He ties her up tight with vines, puts an apple in her mouth, hands behind her back—clasped—lips cursed to use her, *even now you leave me wanting, even though I am never yours.* They aren't so different after all, this firm beginning; a Spring jilted. New rain over soil fresh raked; and even though she hates this, she is widening into a body.

Object Relations

stop/look at these fine tits/got tits
with power now/got tits that speak/but/lips
closed/got tits/shut up I'll tell you/show me
your tits/it doesn't need to mean a thing/shape
of the mouth/choke deep/gagging on tits
love the shape of you/tits/I love you/mounds
let me/love you/send me pictures of your round tits
let me get on with it/bra off/that's good/now
let me look at you/come on/let me/knickers down
let me see/suck tits/come on/put yourself down
pull your legs back/that's how I'll fuck you
you'll love it/stop talking/let's see your tits again
you're a fucking goddess/open your legs/mother lust
blunt/*godish*/your cunt/no place like home/you cunt

Misogyny/Misandry

I hold the mirror up I am the darkness

I hold the mirror up

he says   I am dark

I am the dark   he says

he says   I am the mirror

I am   the dark

You Want This Death?

—not a question so much as the answer
it made sense—standing on the rocks
looking at the moon—knowing love
another strange longing to be filled
enough to let me split—spill—shipwreck
out at sea the tide pulls—sighs
restless and fast as a wife for too long
to writhe again—full sin of this body
whispers which spit at me—jump
writhe again—this body full of sin
fast and restless as a wife for too long
out at sea the tide pulls—sighs
enough to let you spill—split—shipwreck
another strange longing filled
look at the moon—love
made sense—stood on the rocks
not a question so much as the answer
you want this death

Collage

I love the way old paper rips
the ease with which it separates
the tear and peel of edges past
I love the way old creases sing
I tear the days of pages back
I ruin the ripped-up rage of days
I love the way old paper rips
I rip the morning from your chest
and find a paper softness there
I love the way old creases sin
I pull you all the way back now
the ease with which years separate
the rip and peal of pages past
I tear the days right back to then

Asking to See My Arse is Not a Love Poem

You slide   into my DM's   a quick swipe
watch me live and move   fire emojis

you look beautiful   screenshot full of hot
hearts   *I like red lipstick*   *did you do that for me*

what are you wearing underneath   *writing poetry*
about you and silence   *the next Bishop and Lowell*

I would take you to Paris   *not a man's fault*
he could lose himself   *at the beginning of time*

engulfed by lips   *what man wouldn't?*
want to see my cock   *love your arse*

slip off a skirt   *let me read your work*
I grasp   what's left

of my self-respect   *I didn't mean*   *'I love you"*
I meant I love your body   *stop talking dirty bitch*

The Black Hat

I bought you from a market, surprised
you suited me. The blackness, the hatness,
arousing to touch your matte felt.
I allow you to shadow me whole,
though the sun falls mostly on the brim.
I want you, hat. Dressed in you, I want me.
I wear you for years. Send you secret messages,
say my thoughts are gone missing, spilled
like almost-black paints that touch.
I rest you on a luggage rack, leave you
at Crewe—when you separate
with something you didn't choose, you lose
a part of the future you'll never get back,
minutes / lover / door keys / hat.
Funny thing is, without you, hat,
I saw far ahead, the sun on only me,
its fire burning my throat.

whistle

a boy I high kicked with
        at a disco   is dead

he loved to dance   at a party
at his house

he asked me upstairs
        kissed me   quick

eyes rolling back   in his head
I imagined   this must be   what

it is like to kiss   the dead
Sunday morning after   a night before

walking in a trance   with earphones
along the headland rail this preacher's

son is hit by a train   stopped   dead
in his tracks not hearing   the warning

Shell Body

White patterned socks
the ones with holes
pulled up to my knee—
elastic nips
at skin.

Playground grownups;
who's the daddy?
black buckled toes
bulbous shoes scuff
the loose shale.

In the drab yard,
a beetle lands,
bustles wings back
to back. Crawls
to a stillness.

Dark spots on red.
Neil pushes me over,
foot crushing
the shell body
to cud on pits of a stone.

My unsocked knee
gracing gravel. Stone
bites, lost blood
rounds a lip
of flesh-covered grit.

After, at the hospital,
wound washed,
dressed in ticklish tape
the nurse calls
butterfly stitches,

the scar blooms
under, plasters
over, cracks
years with blotched marks.
Boys troubled by beauty.

Nails

Wet play time
in the room
with no window.
The trolley tray
for rainy days
between
concertina doors
I try to pass
as normal.
John Paul Shaw
jolts the rack
into me. Surprise.
I'm winded, wounded.
He pushes,
bending me double
over hopeful crayons,
blank paper, glue.
Tears spring hurt,
raise bile. I move away
seeking safety.
He shoves the tray,
breaks the skin
on hips.
I lurch
forwards, scratch
slicing air, his chin
breaking skin
with uncouth nails.
He bleeds

and I am scolded
by Sister Catherine
who says
I am wild
and entirely
uncut.

The Park

He waited for me outside school,
took me into the barn of a local park.
Kissed me—
first little bites on my bottom lip,
just a valley girl and wayward boy
while outside summer soared—

the sound of bats clicked, crickets
in the grass. White swans on the water,
long necks curved in still reflection
of the next.

                A reputation preceded him.
His real name was Jason
but they called him *Spunkie*.

He slipped my hand down his pants,
pushed me to grasp his gland. *Please—
I won't come inside you.*

No
        I said *no, you won't come inside.*
If I'd have known what was yet to come
from men, I might have let him do it.
Instead I ran out, left him emptying
on the wall he'd just pinned me to—
what was I saving myself for?
I've often wondered how he'd have felt
the glistening tip of him opening me.

Turning 30 in New York

We wake to a breakfast of not talking.
You still have your addiction.
Things won't get better.
Three floors up I watch folks like drops
wetting the sidewalk, and think
of what I haven't had.

A beach in Cancun 10 years earlier,
We won't be this beautiful again.
Laid out in a bikini, sick as a lonely dog.
My tits blown huge and milk veined.
A longing I had to get rid of.
I never did.
                It rains.
I walk for hours through Central Park
in my blue marathon trainers.
You go home as someone else.
I wait for a cab on Brooklyn Bridge.

The edges of wet nights I hang myself on.
Over water, lights promise me nothing.
This distance, a reflection to hold on to.
Fifteen years later we won't talk.

I Shouldn't Have Loved

after Edna St Vincent Millay

I shouldn't have loved you, regretfully;
you made a seagull of me, at best.
Made me *nothing better to see,*
caught my kiss, my thought, my rest.
With petty excuses at your side,
you won me, groomed me to your gaze.
Naked, dressed in shame the size
of legs spread wide. Your wicked ways.
What was I to you? What you declaim,
as one more nightmare, living dream.
You walked with pleasure, what did I gain?
I took desire's road. I'm tired now, I'm mean.
A ghost in memory of a girl you knew
who would have loved you in a day or two.

To an Unborn Daughter

Darling, in a London hotel room I let my book fall,
lie back and look at the ceiling the same colour as
the walls and wait for a hangover, though I haven't
earned one. The years get you like that; rough and
threadbare as a fact. I bleed on slept-in sheets, eat
squared fruit from a plastic tub, make a memoir of
my ghosts, suck them up. A train cuts over the
bridge. The bed rattles. Night falls. I rise. I rise and
the sheet crumples. At the window I see leaves,
soaked roads. Everything moves, quickening
through these red-veined streets. My flesh
cushions the light, shadowed through rain-dashed
glass, splashed off the rooftop, as thoughts of you
dishevel me. I feel homesick for where I never
lived, hungry for what I never held. My fingers
slicked with sentiment. The palm of my hand, an
empty page. In the mirror I met an old woman,
moans on her lips. *Let me have November and my
dead.* My arms full of gifts for you. Hope holds
tight as praying hands, time spreads thin as rain.

deathless

the ceiling is white   *i taste of rain*   he says
as night falls   doink   liquid

on water's flat surface   do i   *know what upsets you*
the answer   *no i don't now i do*   wet gathers

drops slip   doink   *look*
the ceiling is empty   he is   doing tongue

i do nothing   he is whittling fitful
the damp of a spilled hour   grows round

growling black   *watch me watching back*   bloom
my blood knows red   he says   eyes dilate *flavoured*

sweet but wilful   eyes close tight   the rain is coming
through   and there is nothing   but air to hold on to

i'm coming   like light has ended
i'm coming   where water

began   where being pools
just deep enough   to drown

Womb in Night Sky with Broken Heart

Globules of blood congeal on the open heart, brackish with scars and beating with night. Flickers of figures pulse in the void, touching the bruise and tearing the wound. New life, forms in a circle of stars, a tight womb, red, broken. *Come close. Don't close.*

Sliced

can't   think
about a   knife without
thinking   of
          the body the
spine   the knife singing
together   tighter than skin
always   the
knife and   its potential to carve
a bone   one
     holds
        to

How to Winter

Look! See how your dead are coming through the gaps between the wall and door frame, drafts of cold wind on a late December night. Remember how the trees swayed till you thought they would break. The light faded. Yesterday you walked for miles in melted snow, rivers across fields, and felt your legs ache from the ghosts hiding in your knees. Today you can't move. The house keens and groans. Life collapses around you. The sound of a dog's wet snores. The cat and his tapeworm sleep in a purr of dark. The refrigerator hums. Night creeps, tangy as leftovers. Buzzing of another year ending, the downstairs tv, disasters gathered to warm you, still as an hour. The clock pops like a gun.

Sevenling

He loved an empty drawer
a wardrobe door ajar
an open window halfway wide

the dregs of tea now cold
to glimpse the edges of my scar
a part read book left on the side

A cigar is never just a cigar

hyperdulia

my cunt is a wound
you   worship
fuck it   full
devout
unburdened   eden
closes   around   you
my wound is a cunt

Jump

another me is in a room/with you/can only
see it through a mirror reflecting/another photo
in a hand/held/mirror/on a screen/zoom in
here we are/just/one version/you/of me/we
rest/unmade bed/leg fallen/full/spread
hand on shoulder/hair/over you/chest rising
want to sleep/think/this place where no one
shifts/we exist/bliss/breathe out/other selves
escape/the room/break hands/let go
remember a past/a future will not pass/pull
myself apart/one called now/another how do I
get/me/all of me/splits/shudders into
fragments/arriving at/an estuary/jump
another me is saying/sink/another me is
saying mud/might be/cold/another you is
saying mud/another you never/jumped

sonnet XL

for Persephone

in growing darkness i expand/ignite embers
earn my witchness/my wickedness/part
damp earth between found legs/cast a honeyed
split with woven guile/you've looked/lacked/the ache
is mute/the hush has licked me open/black/
our fated minds attract this trick/pull at threads/plot
hungry to unravel/dying to be dead for you/suck
this little ploy that worms through/hands
crave to jolt the middle wound/your voweled
voice spells this sin/flesh made rash/burns mad/
chokes/holds me by the throat/pulls from my body
quick/the foul ghost invoked/every cry tight as a kiss/
cradle my very name over flames/spit wet fevers/
sniff now my dusk/slide stiff over me/surge night/cunny
blacksmith of my remaking/change me/shape me real

Wings

Each night at twilight I will walk
to feel the dark air swooping in
and bats along the river shore,
the water black as rippled silk.

The path leads to worn-out road,
the sun now low and out of sight,
casts pale pink glances back to slight
the total pitchy of the glass.

I don't know how to be alone.
Night air as soft as newborn skin,
the hoot of roosting birds, not named
come calling at this chilly spring.

And if air remembers flight
and time again how much is missed
in filling all the world with light, I
step back now and breathe with wings.

Odradek

*"...the whole thing looks senseless
enough but in its own way perfectly finished."*
- E. Muir on translating Kafka's Odradek

O was someone you ate for breakfast and they were not
scared of you. You made them think of eating oranges in
segments, of sunrises, of when the world will spilt open
with the wound of it. You can hardly look. Drink hot tea
from a mug with a cracked handle. Drink water from a
blue cup. Take the handle off the jug. Tell me the world
will split open. Tell me it will.　　　　　　Tell me.
Sometimes these thoughts are the same colour as light. At
those times you cannot bare to look. Nothing is without
its edges, round as the eyes O will give. The colour of the
setting sun, so beautiful you can barely look. Look
anyway. Look away and you melt into memory. You
knew it was not going to last until morning. Your eyes
close like a blackout blind. It's like putting your hand
into an empty vessel expecting to find　　　　something.

Faith

understanding is a bruise blushing full
under gums and like a liquid it will spread

to face the rest of you and curdle like the smell
of breathless bones, feather-mouthed and juiceless

a dry doll, the last drink a long time gone
bleach ardently spilt on soft white skin

falling through the eager edges ripped
full sun on a tarmac playground you sit

quiet as an A-frame, shushed, a radio
turned on low and lower in the background

It wasn't him

                                    I loved—but me

I made desire real
gentled my touch   body's soft rise—

ripe shine   milk openings

It wasn't his but my green eyes
I longed for   wild with storms

with shadow sighs   night's thick cries
quick little deaths   fire-licked pleas

too much for him—
                            —not too much

for me   fingers run
my split lips   spilt at my own hand

too late   his whispers gone
                            a dark swan

—how still I am   hushed

Achlys

Achlys is with me, her sadness and sorrow. Daimona of the death mist. Her poisons soothe my body to submission. Her clouds fog my eyes in death. Goddess of the eternal night, she fights to keep me in her whitened dark. Wraps her hands around my throat. I put my hands to her neck. She won't choke, has never taken breath. She puts her lips to mine. I struggle against her, but it is futile. She holds me close, sucks my damp air out in one long pull and swallows. And I'd disappear down her throat, if she'd just hold me like that forever. *Let me breathe no more.* But she's letting me go, releasing me from her grey hands and I am born again. My mother witch of chaos throws me out into the light of the world, so blinding that for a time I will beg her, *take me back.*

Winter Treason

after Edna St Vincent Millay

My cold body bowed where it then stood
before your words chastened it. I recall
still longings, chill worlds with hearts of wood,
my ears spilled open. The first to fall,
a deep and constant blunt ache leaves
me darkening, dripping black in nulled sun.
I cannot say what's left behind that grieves
and wrings its hands at what our love has done.
In the widening silence none can guess
the moment known long before first eyes
met. Feasting on your late loneliness,
your body lists into mine with sighs.
Summer's long hours have left the season,
we do not push away this winter treason.

Da

da is looking for his good hat/
/it's difficult to find things/
he thinks I am my mother/
/time unbound into nothing/
it's on the hook in the bedroom da
the hat hung up like a lost dream/

/earlier I cut the unloved
wisps of his grey hair
with blunt scissors/
/felt his body soothe at the touch
of another/warm hands/hot
cloth on old skin/deepening
the shave/stubborn stubble/rusty
blades/*these are the new ones* / he says

.

Ma

I stand by the door/not wanting
/to see my mother/knowing/I have to/
smell my mother's cigarettes/though
it's been months since she was home/
/years since/I have grown closed/
/at the hospital mother doesn't know
who I am/da sits quiet under his hat/
she says/*alleluia* / his eyes say/*hold me*
/he holds her hand still/*what's left here*/
it's all old now/even the hat/

/*How is your alleluia*/ *It's good* / I tell her
/lying/*my alleluia is fine*/she bursts
into song like a baby bird/it's good/
to see her/happy or a plucked thrush/

.

What's Left

In my father's garage,
with and without lids,
every size of jar.
Pieces of string from the war.
Five wonky framed bikes
too low for each grandchild.
His paper-creased hands
wheeling them out.

No room in the car Dad.
His bright eyes.
Two choked chainsaws.
His wisps of hair uncut.
Blunt lawnmower blades.
Our speechless exchange
of found and empty years.
Cut loose with old shears.
I have so much at parting.

Take care love—
as if his words won't last.
As if these words were last.

Maternité

At the Louvre, a mother of boys
cries, a son missing. For hours
his brothers call, over and again
his name. *Cheveux noir, jeans,
green chemise, have you seen him?*
That day we hang on the tram,
follow childless Sunday families
along the *pas de deux* of the Seine,
neck of broken spires, out to
the carved arches of the swan.
Ten stops to Porte de Vannes
as the market stalls are packed up
emptyied plyboard trestles.
Now blankets spread, suitcases
opened side by side with mothers
holding babies tight, unzip bags,
cough up burdens of unlikely gifts.
Mirrors and rings of ended love.
I wish not to be afraid of strangers
selling stories for a meal.
Things thrown down, cast away
with hope, no opulence or waste,
the gap in fate an outlawed cost.
I wonder if the son's still lost.
I long to hold my boys miles away.
On route to Charles de Gaulle,
through Pont de L'alma
where history took the once
most famous mother in its mouth.

Then on and out to Place Dulcie.
Here a stone mother takes
the plume-soft furl of a child's hand
to caress her hard face.

Constellations

for Caroline Hershel*

iPhone torches light the lane
                    white flowers there like stars
                                        moon curbed at a half

we wandered off the path and talked of Leda and the Swan
                                        huge wings of white
holding her down
                    there we stilled
                                        side by side
watching quiet satellites

girls guided by unknowing
                    the sky filled with milky noise
orbs with names of captured Greek brides

                              Cassiopeia   Andromeda   Pleiades
doing penance for impetuousness

immortalised across the open net of almost dark
an overlie of woven stars
                        Sagittarius' bow shot in the arms
                                    the bite of Hercules at the hip
whip of Orion's belt

Ursa bear hunting through the small intestines

                    Ptolemy's pet Pegasus hoofing out a Hippocrene in the blood
Draco's dragon Ladon
                            eating apples off the mound of Venus
Andromeda a soft white light
                        wide mesh of the open sky
                                    holding it all together
the most distant object visible with the eye
                            galaxies draped across shoulders

eyes dizzying on musky shuttles
            space mice wove a white thread line

                                    of unexpected knowing

* All I know, I owe to my brother. I am the tool which he has shaped to his use. *-Caroline Hershel, astronomer, born 1750, her work overshadowed by the lesser discoveries of her brother William.*

The Butter

Is too hard to spread
smears round
into numb pats
will give if pushed
once knew how to slip
between fingers
white milk full-fat
flow of a gland
feeding calves
hungry to know
what it will become.

Take me into the sun
remind me to drip
run through shifts
slope into shape
turn imperfectly
in state—yes— say yes
caught against
hot palms
slick warm knives
tipped cutting
the lid off the world
handfuls of stars
melt into open cracks
sky softens pours
through the gaps.

Wild Figs

afer Mary Oliver & Ellen Bass

You do not have to promise me forever,
do not have to say this will always be
as it is now. You only have to let
yourself be the moment completely.
Hold me, look into my eyes, tell me
you are here now, and for as many nows
as we both consent. Speak truth, push
fingers into my soft skin. Leave a bruise.
The days fall like leaves and winter is near.
Pull close the lonely fruit of my body.
Take me to your chest. Keep me safe
against the surge of your breath, pressing.
Here we are, listen—I offer my heartbeat.
Sometimes, pick me—eat me whole.

Pret a Manger

By Wednesday I'd fallen in love with the city,
its cigarette butts, bus stops, the hopeless parks.

Throbbing steel struts, glass arches, concrete plazas
gaping, sharp spires, flat-bellied bridges.

By the end of the week I'd surrendered my body
let the city take me.

Embankments, escalators, elevators. I was them all,
windows opening reflecting nothing but myself.

Men on mopeds had pieces of my heart
delivered in zipped black bags to the closest bidder.

The gold-tiled steps of each tube edge
absorbed me—rain down gutters,

poured coffee down my throat.
I didn't smudge my lips,

hands no longer in my pockets,
ready to be eaten on every corner.

November 5th 2023

Sky fires of orange and yellow   blunt red
lights up   the little hills
urgent knots of moon   November's
sallow eye as the sky caves   blue
no thing will break   this English sleep
safe on the ground   lost in fulgid dreams
no sirens split   the coming dark
no words   our mouths too full
outside smoke brims the still air   inside
we watch a film   the house rumbles
shakes our lonely bodies   to the news

St Anthony

Hide with me
search in churches
skulk for recluse
sneak in graveyards
under archways
snatched
from the eyes
of all but god
hold me
your hand
pressing thigh
into bone
leave a bruise
open a door
stained light
shattered
who I am
what I'm for
set loose
on mute stone
and then
quiet streets
settle into
a hymn

I
love
love because it is
I don't know how
to love. You—
love you
I love
I

The river felt she wanted salt

after James Joyce
by way of Anselm Kiefer

a stream chilled with hearts gold on triangles love in squared
sheets leaden life of a river stripped with oil the smell of
centuries laid like a rooftop open to the sky the dead sea
woman will water the whole world over and over again
change and fill and empty Adam was a fish and his daughter
was water spilling water spinning earnestly conceived hopes
concrete sunflowers bend then fall around the edges slows the
pace fingerprints in dust I want to lie down curl like the three of
them dressed in black rise like snakes in the remnants of witch
fingers in the dust I want to hide under the ledges fallen to
make holes you will rise if you must ssssssss see the snake
worries every side the first rattle of the universe then breathe
women pour oil on a navel from a hot hand

Blunder

to make a halting quiet in the mind
the only wish you had was time to build
not quickly as want droops beneath the wind
there are so many moments to be killed
the recurring circle as a maker's haste
the waste of yesterday chokes the past
the clocks will always know what's best
moving through endless rooms and corridors
the way you choose unopened doors
those turned away and those your guests
but only once
                    inspire or regret with guilt
monstrous edges that no maker built
but sat beneath a dying tree in shade
all dreams silent, bound to fade.

Cooper Red
(10x8)

after Anselm Kiefer

small human in a square jar	unfilled space surrounds
life	all the dried roses
garlands of water	dragged along the riverbed
dried roses	and Cooper Red
	sheen of a golden fleece
archive	of memory
saltwater　　is dead	splash of　　molten grey
hidden in rags	squash me in woman
reflections of light	will　　as a wave
open a lid	empty the jar
there the soggy bones	arms stuck to the sides

No running

The double red-lipped
rings of my coffee cup.
The mirrored moons
of my nails, pink-eyed
with tight white.
How hard
it was to walk away
holding the morning.
Longing to be held
in bigger arms.
The reflection
of seven heads
in the glass-
framed portrait
We watched
each other
through a screen
unsharpened.
The ash
of last night's fire.
The moon low,
longing to be held,
crisp white.
Somethings are meant
to be kept outside.
How hard it was
to walk away.
We watched each other, how hard it was,
to walk away,
a swans neck
curves back
towards the heart.

Muse

I met her once, leant over
my bed as I slept
an unrestful sleep, her breath
hot, wet in my ear, she screamed
her face a nest of wrinkles
netted with years, opened
her mouth, no words came out—
bees in the thatch, splitting stones,
the hard talk of a new guest
at the long table—
wake up, her grey hair trailed
she spat in my face like fire
and cold, nowhere to go
but to my bones.

Her smile like mud,
hairs on my skin rising.
Her mouth rousing a sinkhole,
Say something. Need. Break
your heart,
let it bleed.

And I Drove My Car

I drove my car off the edge of the world. My foot on the break and I didn't stop. I didn't stop falling. The falling was sweet like grass watered all summer and soft underfoot. I fell out through the bottom of my life, looked back to see a kaleidescope through the rearview. The split truth of my life thrust at me, splintered into a lovely hue of blue-green. I drove my car through all this turquoise *apocalypse*, this navy *armageddon*. Falling until the falling became a circle, a mantra, an eternal azure tunnel over a motorway bridge. And I'm driving across water now, over the end of everything. All the things I ever felt, I'm above them now, watching it flow under me and the world like a light-up lamp in the distance. All that love, all that hate and I drove my car right over it. Like it didn't even matter anymore. I just kept on driving. I stayed in the car melancholic and drove, put Billy Joel on the speakers and I didn't give a fuck about the bills. I thought of all the missing hits then, the music made me sad. That nothing, the space between who I was and who I am. Then Boom. Wham. Everything quickly. An explosion on the bridge over the earth and I'm in all the pieces of myself. Fuck Billy Joel. All the little pieces falling, falling. Off the edge of the world. A dust cloud. Now I'm spinning all the pieces of myself in a cerulean nebula, a baby blue universe unborn and made up of a particular dust. All the little grey dust motes through a wide lens, opening. I'm taking it all in.

Between Me and the White Fire of the Stars

after Mary Oliver

I laid myself down in soil,
rich soil like you wouldn't believe—
full of the blood of my women,
mother, grandmothers, daughter
lost in water and bone.
For hours I heard my tears,
my fears whispered in sobs,
I laid myself down and wept in earth.
Drenched my black skirts, pockets
full of moth. But night is coming
and it is time. I do my work
in the dark. Kingdoms fall,
rivers are nothing but forgotten.
Little birds fly at dusk.
Before dawn I am perfect,
I've eaten the skin off myself.
A moon, tasted and waned,
whole, wasting none. More!
I wake like never before—
come out and see the stars.

We came forth and once more saw the stars.

-Canto XXXIV, Dante's *Inferno*

Part II

Love led us both to share in one death.

-Canto V, Dante's *Inferno*

I Did Love You Once

-Hamlet. William Shakespeare.

He didn't come to the lake.
Said he would. Said he couldn't.
She feels it then. She won't be read
again. The Fates pull their own hair.
The book's pages fall. Ripped
to the water, left wetted. Sink dirty.
She shivers. Closes. Imagines
a wound with arms unfolded,
holding her. *It was lonely before—*
she'd have said *kiss me edgeless*
reading the words to him, last brawl
of their shattered art. Each line cold
and glassy sharp as the last. Lost star—
no chance now of something good.
Be all my sins remembered.

This Perverse Heart*

1.

[last night]   [opened]
[broke]   [my heart]

[or perhaps a bridge]

    [for love *beyond the rubble of the world*]

      [fixed with rusted nails to struts]

[where else should love meet]

[running without a backwards glance]

[navigating by the stars]   [the night betrayed]

      [enormous and stirring]

2.

[entering]   [almost touching]

[*at the centre of a dream*]

[more than the last]

                          [the same frayed smile]

[I devour twitching]

3.

[full moon sweat]

[tell me against the cold]

[your hands transform me]

[finger of night naming itself]

[tell me]   [let me see]

[pause to watch]   [I devour twitching]

[the same frayed smile]

[unhitched through the dark]

4.

[our bodies still glowing]   [naked and shivering]

[your hands transform me]

[body clasped]

[this burlesque speechless]   [pack of disguises]

[my words on your back]

                              [in teeth and blood}

[I have no mouth]

                         [through darkness without spirit]

5.

[we splash upon the sheets]

[light seeps from us]

[tell me]

[pulse racing]   [never let up]

[a finger's warmth curls with lies]

[stiff with salt]

[instead of a kiss you leave]

6.

[only the words have gone]

[darkness]   [a friend]

[where we are not yet born]

7.

[held in darkness]

[trick of living invisible]

[half remembered]   [murmur of wind]

[flux of sleep washes]   [sighs]   [stung with sun]

[wiping up the surface of the moon]

[filling each room]

8.

[spreading}   [surface seething]

[last night melts empty]

[up to the elbows]

[you pull away]   [want me]

[ask me]

9.

[you are in love with sunlight}

[I have only this breath]

[ancient and sleepy]

[gibberish with feathers]

[shrugging]   [*at the moment of the kill*]

[holding the neck with shaking hands]

[to make a significance]

10.

[roundness of a swan neck]   [isolated grace]

[over my body]   [you watch me]

[see me]   [explosion of looking]

[object to be perceived]   [feathered]

[the sound of a word]

[cunt]   [swan fuck]

[keep the bird dead]

[bend the shapely neck]

11.

[fearful of ever finding]

        [a human document]

    [dog eared as love]

12.

[I have no words]   [look at all my words]

[rip up the paper]   [wet the pages]

13.

[evening will come again]   [wasteful and selfish]

[we will sleep]

14.

[seeing you seeing me]   [formless]

[looking at you looking]

[burning]   [hands down my back]

[place them over my ears]

[touch me]   [don't touch me]

[place them over me while I sleep]

[can you see me]   [tell me]

[do you see me]

[I get to the light]   [through your darkness]

[I see you]   [please hold me]   [   ]

15.

[close to you]

[finishings of filth]   [I have to go]

[tongue out]

[known limits of the mouth]

                              [I have no mouth]

[funny thing] [I am]

[made up of faces]

[how long]

                    [you throw this elegant solution]

            [bee stung lips]

[how long]

[your ear caught on the phone]

16.

[all things with wild tumult]

[that she loves you]   [tell me]

[the love was broken when I wore it]

[we threw it away]

[the love was already broken when I tore it]

17.

[I look at myself beneath us]

[we enter a box]

[escaping the sky]   [nothing else]

[that she loves you]   [with debts]

[not talking now]

[just looking]   [now]

                    [later we will think]

18.

[curved meat]   [swan]   [unaltered by maps]

[no constellations]   [only chance]

[straight away look]   [and after watch it]

[look]   [look]   [dead]

[raise up a black heart]

[underground]   [invisible]

[headlong rush]   [the walls choking]

[adulthood puddles]   [edges failed]

[are you awake]

19.

[drive me away in your car]

[only the sea lays down again]

[I put my head down in your car]

[your hands are cold]

[little love]   [who made you like this]

[stalk]   [brave]   [turbulent bird]

[but I noticed]   [I need time]

[where to look]   [to tell lies]

[stillness can be true]   [where do we draw the line]

[stay down on me]

20.

[like a man's supposed to be held]

[you've come]   [white lipped with luck]

[we have exhausted words]

21.

[to join again]

[underneath the bed]

[to have suffered]   [with the black light]

[undiminished thirst]

[weakness rasps out an absence]

[you want me again]   [what are you wearing]

22.

[who is playing now]

[understand who is playing]

[or what we are]   [do]

[beyond]   [love and hate]

[no time to play]   [I wanted you]

                    [there was no time]

23.

[I am shaken}

             [moving]   [I'm going to go]

[man plus] [womanless]   [undone]

[the price of looking]

[in darkness]   [instead for whores]

[we meet behind glass]

             [this *perverse heart*]

[you *pitch down* with one unreasonable finger]

24.

[short *blunt* text]   [sex]

[*trigger finger* catastrophe]   [is of course fear]

[we are given names we outgrow]

[thirst is a peace we make]

25.

                                        [let me enter]

[bend over]   [to catch a whisper]

[silent as a stranger]

            [inside me]

[a smell of burning]   [all roads returning]

[it is my heart]

[my ghosts]   [far from]   [men's eyes]

26.

[   ]

[an island]

[a room]

[a womb]   [not yet born]

[break me]

                                                       [into being]

[   ]

[I'm coming]   [containing myself]

[here is my mouth]

                                                       [I have disappeared]

[to be held]   [behold]

[leave the tomb]   ] open [

[what are you wearing?   ]

27.

[the gap no longer holds]

[aching to fuck]

[slutch in my fingers]   [failing to catch]

[the ache in my heart]

[I am unfound]   [ungrounded]

[we touch] [like mud
                    ]

[there you are
          ]

                                        here I am

---

*Note on the poem text: 'This Perverse Heart' is an exploration of the tragic entanglement of Hamlet and Ophelia, in which the affection of one for the other is continually lost in the disjointed communication between them. A few words within the weave of these fragments originate from 'A Smell of Burning' by Thomas Blackburn, 1961. Putnam Press, London. These are indicated by the use of italics. The title of this poem is inspired by a line from Blackburn's poem 'Soho Nights'.

ACKNOWLEDGEMENTS

'whistle' appeared in *Poetry Wales Spring 2023* in Welsh
'womb in night sky' is forthcoming in the *Best of Newcastle Anthology 2024*

With huge thanks to Stuart at Verve; Tamar Yoseloff for top-notch editing again; to my endorsers: novelist Paul Lynch and poets Luke Kennard, Meryl Pugh and Ophira Adar. Endless gratitude to my writing family 'The Jugs'. And finally thank you to The Poetry School and Arvon for all the wonderful teachers past and present who have given me the truest gift of a writing education.

Eighty Four:

Poems on Male Suicide, Vulnerability, Grief and Hope

With an introduction from editor Helen Calcutt

Eighty Four was originally a new anthology of poetry on the subject of male suicide in aid of CALM. Poems were donated to the collection by Andrew McMillan, Salena Godden, Anthony Anaxogorou, Katrina Naomi, Ian Patterson, Caroline Smith, Carrie Etter, Peter Raynard, Joelle Taylor, while a submissions window yielded many excellent poems on the subject from hitherto unknown poets we are thrilled to have been made aware of.

We hope this book will shed light on an issue that is cast in shadow, and which is often shrouded in secrecy and denial. If we don't talk, we don't heal and we don't change. In Eighty Four we are all talking. Are you listening?

Available in paperback:
ISBN: 978 1 912565 13 9
188 pages • 216 x 138 • 56 poems
£11.99

And on eBook:
ISBN: 978 1 912565 79 5
£6.99

Where Else:

An International Hong Kong Poetry Anthology

With an introduction from the editors Jennifer Wong, Jason Eng Hun Lee & Tim Tim Cheng

Featuring both established and emerging Hong Kong poets across generations and continents, this unique anthology offers a glimpse into an exciting, diverse range of voices that make up the diasporic imagination of the contemporary Hong Kong poetry community. Adopting a diasporic approach, the anthology encompasses both native Hong Kong writers as well as expatriate and mixed-race voices who were born or have lived in the city.

'We are Hong Kongers to the core and will defend our cantankerous vivid imagination against all invaders and occupiers. Our poetry is the ultimate expression of freedom and is a harbinger of all that is wondrous!' - Marilyn Chin

Available in paperback:
ISBN: 978 1 913917 36 4
252 pages • 216 x 138 • 106 poems
£14.99

And on eBook:
ISBN: 978 1 913917 79 1
£9.99

ABOUT VERVE POETRY PRESS

Verve Poetry Press is a prize-winning press that focused initially on meeting a local need in Birmingham - a need for the vibrant poetry scene here in Brum to find a way to present itself to the poetry world via publication. Co-founded by Stuart Bartholomew and Amerah Saleh, it now publishes poets from all corners of the UK - poets that speak to the city's varied and energetic qualities and will contribute to its many poetic stories.

Added to this is a colourful pamphlet series, many featuring poets who have performed at our sister festival - and a poetry show series which captures the magic of longer poetry performance pieces by festival alumni such as Polarbear and Imogen Stirling.

The press has been voted Most Innovative Publisher at the Saboteur Awards, and has won the Publisher's Award for Poetry Pamphlets at the Michael Marks Awards.

Like the festival, we strive to think about poetry in inclusive ways and embrace the multiplicity of approaches towards this glorious art.

www.vervepoetrypress.com
@VervePoetryPres
mail@vervepoetrypress.com